BROADMAN
&HOLMAN
PUBLISHERS

Students seeking to know God better
through Jesus Christ

The Well is a DePaul Student Religious Organization. We emphasize developing a closer relationship with Christ and fellow students.

Wednesday Night Worship Meeting
DePaul Student Center (Reflection Room 101) 8-9pm

For more information about The Well or to discuss this book, please contact:
Chad Lewis: 773-463-2621, clewis4@depaul.edu
Student Contact: Andrew Roop: 312-498-5375
www.depaul.edu/~thewell

By C. S. Lewis

The Abolition of Man

Mere Christianity

The Great Divorce

The Problem of Pain

The Weight of Glory and Other Addresses

The Screwtape Letters (with ''Screwtape Proposes a Toast'')

Miracles

The Case for Christianity

The Lion, the Witch and the Wardrobe

Prince Caspian

The Voyage of the Dawn Treader

The Silver Chair

The Magician's Nephew

The Horse and His Boy

The Last Battle

Perelandra

That Hideous Strength

Out of the Silent Planet

The Joyful Christian

The Visionary Christian

George Macdonald: An Anthology

C. S. Lewis: Letters to Children,
edited by Lyle W. Dorsett and Marjorie Lamp Mead

*They Stand Together: The Letters of C. S. Lewis to
Arthur Greeves (1914–1963),* edited by Walter Hooper

The Essential C. S. Lewis, edited by Lyle W. Dorsett

THE
CASE FOR
CHRISTIANITY

C. S. Lewis

BROADMAN
&HOLMAN
PUBLISHERS
Nashville, Tennessee

A TOUCHSTONE BOOK
PUBLISHED BY SIMON & SCHUSTER
NEW YORK LONDON TORONTO
SYDNEY TOKYO SINGAPORE

This edition produced by Simon & Schuster, and is distributed to the Christian Bookselling Association by Broadman & Holman Publishers.

TOUCHSTONE
Rockefeller Center
1230 Avenue of the Americas
New York, NY 10020

First Touchstone Edition 1996

TOUCHSTONE and colophon are registered trademarks
of Simon & Schuster Inc.

Manufactured in the United States of America

7   9   10   8   6

Library of Congress Cataloging-in-Publication Data
Lewis, C. S. (Clive Staples), 1898–1963.
The case for Christianity / by C. S. Lewis.
p.   cm.
"Published in England under title: Broadcast talks."
Previously published: New York: Macmillan, 1943.
1. Christianity.   2. Ethics.   I. Title.
BR123.L482   1989   89-9731   CIP
230—dc20
ISBN 0-8054-2044-4

Published in Great Britain as *Broadcast Talks.*

Preface

I GAVE these talks, not because I am anyone in particular, but because I was asked to do so. I think they asked me chiefly for two reasons: firstly, because I am a layman, not a clergyman; and secondly, because I had been a non-Christian for many years. It was thought that both these facts might enable me to understand the difficulties that ordinary people feel about the subject. I am Church of England now myself, but I have tried to put nothing into the second series of talks which all Christians of all Churches do not agree with. With this in view, I sent the script to four clergymen (one Church of England, one Roman Catholic, one Presbyterian, and one Methodist) before they were given on the air. The Church of England man and the Presbyterian agreed with me throughout. The Roman Catholic thought I went too far about the comparative unimportance of *theories* of the "Atonement" in the fourth talk of the second series, and the Methodist would have liked more about Faith in the fifth talk of that series. Both these differences you will find noted when you come to the place. Apart from those, I believe you can take what is said in the second series as plain Christianity which no Christian disagrees with. The first series, of course, does not get as far as Christian doctrines; it is more what might be called philosophy.

C. S. LEWIS.

MAGDALEN COLLEGE.

Contents

PART I

PART II

Part I

RIGHT AND WRONG AS A CLUE TO THE MEANING OF THE UNIVERSE

1

EVERY ONE has heard people quarrelling. Sometimes it sounds funny and sometimes it sounds merely unpleasant; but however it sounds, I believe we can learn something very important from listening to the kind of things they say. They say things like this: "That's my seat, I was there first"—"Leave him alone, he isn't doing you any harm"—"Why should you shove in first?"—"Give me a bit of your orange, I gave you a bit of mine"—"How'd you like it if anyone did the same to you?"—"Come on, you promised." People say things like that every day, educated people as well as uneducated, and children as well as grown-ups.

Now what interests me about all these remarks is that the man who makes them isn't just saying that the other man's behaviour doesn't happen to please him. He is appealing to some kind of standard of behaviour which he expects the other man to know about. And the other man very seldom replies, "To hell with your standard." Nearly always he tries to make out that what he has been doing doesn't really go against the standard, or that if it does, there is some special excuse. He pretends there is some special reason in this particular case why the person who took the seat first should not keep it, or that things were quite different when he was given the bit of orange, or that something has turned up which lets him off keeping his promise. It looks, in fact, very much as if both parties had in mind some kind of Law or

Rule of fair play or decent behaviour or morality or whatever you like to call it, about which they really agreed. And they have. If they hadn't, they might, of course, fight like animals, but they couldn't *quarrel* in the human sense of the word. Quarrelling means trying to show that the other man's in the wrong. And there'd be no sense in trying to do that unless you and he had some sort of agreement as to what Right and Wrong are; just as there'd be no sense in saying that a footballer had committed a foul unless there was some agreement about the rules of football.

Now this Law or Rule about Right and Wrong used to be called the Law of Nature. Nowadays, when we talk of the "laws of nature" we usually mean things like gravitation, or heredity, or the laws of chemistry. But when the older thinkers called the Law of Right and Wrong the Law of Nature, they really meant the Law of *Human* Nature. The idea was that, just as falling stones are governed by the law of gravitation and chemicals by chemical laws, so the creature called man also had *his* law—with this great difference, that the stone couldn't choose whether it obeyed the law of gravitation or not, but a man could choose either to obey the Law of Human Nature or to disobey it. They called it Law of Nature because they thought that every one knew it by nature and didn't need to be taught it. They didn't mean, of course, that you mightn't find an odd individual here and there who didn't know it, just as you find a few people who are colour-blind or have no ear for a tune. But taking the race as a whole, they thought that the human idea of Decent Behaviour was obvious to every one. And I believe they were right. If they weren't, then all the things we say about this war are nonsense. What is the sense in saying the enemy are in the wrong unless Right is a real thing which the Germans

4

at bottom know as well as we do and ought to practise? If they had no notion of what we mean by right, then, though we might still have to fight them, we could no more blame them for that than for the colour of their hair.

I know that some people say the idea of a Law of Nature or decent behaviour known to all men is unsound, because different civilisations and different ages have had quite different moralities. But they haven't. They have only had *slightly* different moralities. Just think what a *quite* different morality would mean. Think of a country where people were *admired* for running away in battle, or where a man felt *proud* for double-crossing all the people who had been kindest to him. You might just as well try to imagine a country where two and two made five. Men have differed as regards what people you ought to be unselfish to—whether it was only your own family, or your fellow countrymen, or every one. But they have always agreed that you oughtn't to put yourself first. Selfishness has never been admired. Men have differed as to whether you should have one wife or four. But they have always agreed that you mustn't simply have any woman you liked.

But the most remarkable thing is this. Whenever you find a man who says he doesn't believe in a real Right and Wrong, you will find the same man going back on this a moment later. He may break his promise to you, but if you try breaking one to him he'll be complaining "It's not fair" before you can say Jack Robinson. A nation may say treaties don't matter; but then, next minute, they spoil their case by saying that the particular treaty they want to break was an unfair one. But if treaties don't matter, and if there's no such things as Right and Wrong—in other words, if there is no Law of Nature—what is the difference between a fair treaty and an unfair one? Haven't they given away the fact that, whatever they say, they really know the Law of Nature just like anyone else?

It seems, then, we are forced to believe in a real Right and Wrong. People may be sometimes mistaken about them, just as people sometimes get their sums wrong; but they are not a matter of mere taste and opinion any more than the multiplication table. Now if we're agreed about that, I go on to my next point, which is this. None of us are really keeping the Law of Nature. If there are any exceptions among you, I apologise to them. They'd better switch on to another station, for nothing I'm going to say concerns them. And now, turning to the ordinary human beings who are left:

I hope you won't misunderstand what I'm going to say. I'm not preaching, and Heaven knows I'm not pretending that I'm better than anyone else. I'm only trying to call attention to a fact; the fact that this year, or this month, or, more likely, this very day, we have failed to practise ourselves the kind of behaviour we expect from other people. There may be all sorts of excuses for us. That time you were so unfair to the children was when you were very tired. That slightly shady business about the money—the one you've almost forgotten—came when you were very hard up. And what you promised to do for old So-and-so and have never done—well, you never would have promised if you'd known how frightfully busy you were going to be. And as for your behaviour to your wife (or husband), if I knew how irritating they could be, I wouldn't wonder at it—and who the dickens am I, anyway? I am just the same. That is to say, I don't succeed in keeping the Law of Nature very well, and the moment anyone tells me I'm not keeping it, there starts up in my mind a string of excuses as long as your arm. The question at the moment is not whether they are good excuses. The point is that they are one more proof of how deeply, whether we like it or not, we believe in the Law of Nature. If we didn't believe in decent behaviour, why should we be so anxious to make excuses for not having behaved decently? The truth is, we believe in decency so much—we feel the Rule or Law pressing on us so—that we can't bear to face the fact that we're breaking it, and consequently we try to shift the responsibility. For you notice that it's only for our bad behaviour that we find all these explanations. We put our *bad* temper down to being tired or worried or hungry; we put our good temper down to ourselves.

Well, those are the two points I wanted to make tonight. First, that human beings, all over the earth, have this curious idea that they *ought* to behave in a certain way, and can't really get rid of it. Secondly, that they don't in fact behave in that way. They know the Law of Nature; they break it. These two facts are the foundation of all clear thinking about ourselves and the universe we live in.

II

If they are the foundation, I had better stop to make that foundation firm before I go on. Some of the letters I have had from listeners show that a good many people find it difficult to understand just what this Law of Human Nature, or Moral Law, or Rule of Decent Behaviour is.

For example, some people write to me saying, "Isn't what

7

you call the Moral Law simply our herd instinct and hasn't it been developed just like all our other instincts?" Now I don't deny that we may have a herd instinct: but that isn't what I mean by the Moral Law. We all know what it feels like to be prompted by instinct—by mother love, or sexual instinct, or the instinct for food. It means you feel a strong want or desire to act in a certain way. And, of course, we sometimes do feel just that sort of desire to help another person: and no doubt that desire is due to the herd instinct. But feeling a desire to help is quite different from feeling that you ought to help whether you want to or not. Supposing you hear a cry for help from a man in danger. You will probably feel two desires—one a desire to give help (due to your herd instinct), the other a desire to keep out of danger (due to the instinct for self-preservation). But you will find inside you, in addition to these two impulses, a third thing which tells you that you ought to follow the impulse to help, and suppress the impulse to run away. Now this thing that judges between two instincts, that decides which should be encouraged, can't itself be either of them. You might as well say that the sheet of music which tells you, at a given moment, to play one note on the piano and not another, is itself one of the notes on the keyboard. The Moral Law is, so to speak, the tune we've got to play: our instincts are merely the keys.

Another way of seeing that the Moral Law is not simply one of our instincts is this. If two instincts are in conflict, and there is nothing in a creature's mind except those two instincts, obviously the stronger of the two must win. But at those moments when we are most conscious of the Moral Law, it usually seems to be telling us to side with the weaker of the two impulses. You probably *want* to be safe much more than you want to help the man who is drowning: but the Moral Law tells you to help him all the same. And doesn't it often tell us to try to make the right impulse stronger than it naturally is? I mean, we often feel it our duty to stimulate the herd instinct, by waking up our imaginations and arousing our pity and so on, so as to get up enough steam for doing the right thing. But surely we are not acting *from* instinct when we set about making an instinct stronger than it is? The thing that says to you, "Your herd instinct is asleep. Wake it up," can't itself *be* the herd instinct. The thing that tells you which note on the piano needs to be played louder can't itself be that note!

Here is a third way of seeing it. If the Moral Law was one of our instincts, we ought to be able to point to some one impulse inside us which was always what we call "good," always in agreement with the rule of right behaviour. But you can't. There is none of our impulses which the Moral Law won't sometimes tell us to suppress, and none which it won't sometimes tell us to encourage. It is a mistake to think that some of our impulses—say, mother love or patriotism—are good, and others, like sex or the fighting instinct, are bad. All we mean is that the occasions on which the fighting instinct or the sexual desire need to be restrained are rather more frequent than those for restraining mother love or patriotism. But there are situations in which it is the duty of a married man to encourage his sexual impulse and of a soldier to encourage the fighting instinct. There are also occasions on which a mother's love for her own children or a man's love for his own country have to be suppressed or they'll lead to unfairness towards other people's children or countries. Strictly speaking, there aren't such things as good and bad impulses. Think once again of a piano. It hasn't got two kinds of notes on it, the "right" notes and the "wrong" ones. Every single note is right at one time and wrong at another. The Moral Law isn't any one instinct or any set of instincts: it is something which makes a kind of tune (the tune we call goodness or right conduct) by directing the instincts.

By the way, this point is of great practical consequence. The most dangerous thing you can do is to take any one impulse of your own nature and set it up as the thing you ought to follow at all costs. There's not one of them which won't make us into devils if we set it up as an absolute guide. You might think love of humanity in general was safe, but it isn't. If you leave out justice you'll find yourself breaking agreements and faking evidence in trials "for the sake of humanity," and become in the end a cruel and treacherous man.

Other people write to me saying, "Isn't what you call the Moral Law just a social convention, something that is put into us by education?" I think there is a misunderstanding here. The people who ask that question are usually taking it for granted that if we have learned a thing from parents and teachers, then that thing must be merely a human invention. But, of course, that isn't so. We all learned the multiplication table at school. A child who grew up alone on a desert island wouldn't know it. But surely it doesn't follow that the multiplication table is simply a human convention, something human beings have made up for themselves and might have made different if they had liked? *Of course* we learn the Rule of Decent Behaviour from parents and teachers, as we learn everything else. But some of the things we learn are mere convention which might have been different —we learn to keep to the left of the road, but it might just as well have been the rule to keep to the right—and others of them, like mathematics, are real truths. The question is which class the Law of Human Nature belongs to.

There are two reasons for saying it belongs to the same class as mathematics. The first is, as I said last time, that though there are differences between the moral ideas of one time or country and those of another, the differences aren't really very big—you can recognise the same Law running through them all: whereas mere conventions—like the rule of the road or the kind of clothes people wear—differ completely. The other reason is this. When you think about these differences between the morality of one people and another, do you think that the morality of one people is ever better or worse than that of another? Have any of the changes been improvements? If not, then of course there could never be any moral progress. Progress means not just changing, but changing for the better. If no set of moral ideas were truer or better than any other there would be no sense in preferring civilised morality to savage morality, or Christian morality to Nazi morality. In fact, of course, we all do believe that some moralities *are* better than others. We do believe that some of the people who tried to change the moral ideas of their own age were what we'd call Reformers or Pioneers—people who understood morality better than their neighbours did. Very well then. The moment you say that one set of moral ideas can be better than another, you are, in fact, measuring them both by a standard, saying that one of them conforms to that standard more nearly than the other. But the standard that measures two things is something different from either. You are, in fact, comparing them both with some Real Morality, admitting that there is *really* such a thing as Right, independent of what people think, and that some people's ideas get nearer to that real Right than others. Or put it this way. If your moral ideas can be truer, and those of the Nazis less true, there must be something—some Real Morality—for them to be true *about*. The reason why your idea of New York can be truer or less true than mine is that New York is a real place, existing quite apart from what either of us thinks. If when each of us said "New York" each meant merely "The town I am imagining in my own head," how could one of us have truer ideas than the other? There'd be no question of truth or falsehood at all. In the same way, if the Rule of Decent Behaviour meant simply, "whatever each nation happens to approve," there'd be no sense in saying that any one nation had ever been more correct in its approval than any other; no sense in saying that the world could ever grow better or worse.

So you see that though the differences between people's ideas of Decent Behaviour often make you suspect that there is no real natural Law of Behaviour at all, yet the things we are bound to think about these differences really prove just the opposite. But one word before I end. I think that some listeners have been exaggerating the differences, because they have not distinguished between differences of morality and differences of belief about facts. For example, one listener wrote and said, "Three hundred years ago people in England were putting witches to death. Was that what you call the Rule of Human Nature or Right Conduct?" But surely the reason we don't execute witches is that we don't believe there are such things. If we did—if we really thought that there were people going about who had sold themselves to the devil and received supernatural powers from him in return and were using these powers to kill their neighbours or drive them mad or bring bad weather, surely we'd all agree that if anyone deserved the death penalty, then these

12

filthy quislings did? There's no difference of moral principle here: the difference is simply about matter of fact. It may be a great advance in *knowledge* not to believe in witches: there's no moral advance in not executing them when you don't think they are there! You wouldn't call a man humane for ceasing to set mouse-traps if he did so because he believed there were no mice in the house.

III

I NOW go back to what I said at the end of the first talk, that there were two odd things about the human race. First, that they were haunted by the idea of a sort of behaviour they ought to practise, what you might call fair play, or decency, or morality, or the Law of Nature. Second, that they didn't in fact do so. Now some of you may wonder why I called this odd. It may seem to you the most natural thing in the world. In particular, you may have thought I was rather hard on the human race. After all, you may say, what I call breaking the Law of Right and Wrong or of Nature, only means that people aren't perfect. And why on earth should I expect them to be? Well, that would be a good answer if what I was trying to do was to fix the exact amount of blame which is due to us for not behaving as we expect others to behave. But that isn't my job at all. I'm not concerned at present with blame; I'm trying to find out truth. And from that point of view the very idea of something being imperfect, of its not being what it ought to be, has certain consequences.

If you take a thing like a stone or a tree, it is what it is and there's no sense in saying it ought to have been otherwise. Of course you may say a stone's "the wrong shape" if you want to use it for a rockery, or that a tree's a bad tree because it doesn't give you as much shade as you expected. But all you mean is that the stone or the tree doesn't happen to be convenient for some purpose of your own. You're not, except as a joke, blaming them for that. You really know that, given the weather and the soil, the tree *couldn't* have been any different. What we, from our point of view, call a "bad" tree is obeying the laws of its nature, just as much as a "good" one.

Now have you noticed what follows? It follows that what we usually call the laws of nature—the way weather works on a tree, for example—may not really be *laws* in the strict sense, but only in a manner of speaking. When you say that falling stones always obey the law of gravitation, isn't this much the same as saying that the law only means "what stones always do"? You don't really think that when a stone is let go, it suddenly remembers that it is under orders to fall to the ground! You only mean that, in fact, it *does* fall. In other words, you can't be sure that there is anything over and above the facts themselves, any law about what ought to happen, as distinct from what does happen. The laws of nature, as applied to stones or trees, may only mean "what Nature, in fact, does." But if you turn to the Law of Human Nature, the Law of Decent Behaviour, it's a different matter. That law certainly doesn't mean "what human beings, in fact, do"; for as I said before, many of them don't obey this law at all, and none of them obey it completely. The law of gravity tells you what stones do if you drop them; but the Law of Human Nature tells you what human beings ought to do, and don't. In other words, when you're dealing with humans, something else comes in above and beyond the actual facts. You have the facts (how men do behave) and you also have something else (how they ought to behave). In the rest of the universe there needn't be anything but the facts. Electrons and molecules behave in a certain way, and certain results follow, and that *may* be the whole story.[1] But men behave in a certain way and that's not the whole story, for all the time you know that they ought to behave differently.

Now this is really so peculiar that one is tempted to try to explain it away. For instance, we might try to make out that when you say a man oughtn't to act as he does, you only mean the same as when you say that a stone's the wrong shape; namely, that what he's doing happens to be inconvenient to you. But that just isn't true. A man occupying the corner seat in the train because he got there first, and a man who slipped into it while my back was turned and removed my bag, are both equally inconvenient. But I blame the second man and don't blame the first. I'm not angry— except perhaps for a moment before I came to my senses— with a man who trips me up by accident; I am angry with a man who tries to trip me up even if he doesn't succeed. Yet the first has hurt me and the second hasn't. Sometimes the behaviour which I call bad is not inconvenient to me at all, but the very opposite. In war, each side may find a traitor on the other side very useful. But though they use him and pay him they regard him as human vermin. So you can't say that what we call decent behaviour in others is simply the behaviour that happens to be useful to us. And as for decent

[1] I don't think it *is* the whole story, as you will see later. I mean that, as far as the argument has gone up to date, it *may* be.

15

behaviour in ourselves, I suppose it's pretty obvious that it doesn't mean the behaviour that pays. It means things like being content with thirty shillings when you might have got three pounds, leaving a girl alone when you'd like to make love to her, staying in dangerous places when you could go somewhere safer, keeping promises you'd rather not keep, and telling the truth even when it makes you look a fool.

Some people say that though decent conduct doesn't mean what pays each particular person at a particular moment, still, it means what pays the human race as a whole; and that consequently there's no mystery about it. Human beings, after all, have some sense; they see that you can't have any real safety or happiness except in a society where every one plays fair, and it's because they see this that they try to behave decently. Now, of course, it's perfectly true that safety and happiness can only come from individuals, classes, and nations being honest and fair and kind to each other. It is one of the most important truths in the world. But as an explanation of why we feel as we do about Right and Wrong it just misses the point. If we ask, "Why ought I to be unselfish?" and you reply, "Because it is good for society," we may then ask, "Why should I care what's good for society except when it happens to pay *me* personally?" and then you'll have to say, "Because you ought to be unselfish" —which simply brings us back to where we started. You're saying what's true, but you're not getting any further. If a man asked what was the point of playing football, it wouldn't be much good saying, "in order to score goals," for trying to score goals is the game itself, not the reason for the game, and you'd really only be saying that football was football— which is true, but not worth saying. In the same way, if a man asks what is the point of behaving decently, it's no good replying, "in order to benefit society," for trying to benefit other people, in other words being unselfish is one of the things decent behaviour consists in; all you're really saying is that decent behaviour is decent behaviour. You'd have said just as much if you'd stopped at the statement, "Men ought to be unselfish."

And that's just where I do stop. Men ought to be unselfish, ought to be fair. Not that men are unselfish, nor that they like being unselfish, but that they ought to be. The Moral Law, or Law of Human Nature, is not simply a fact about human behaviour in the same way as the Law of Gravitation is, or may be, simply a fact about how heavy objects behave. On the other hand, it's not a mere fancy, for we can't get rid of the idea, and most of the things we say and think about men would be reduced to nonsense if we did. And it's not simply a statement about how we should like men to behave for our own convenience; for the behaviour we call bad or unfair isn't exactly the same as the behaviour we find inconvenient, and may even be the opposite. Consequently, this Rule of Right and Wrong, or Law of Human Nature, or whatever you call it, must somehow or other be a real thing—a thing that's really there, not made up by ourselves. And yet it's not a fact in the ordinary sense, in the same way as our actul behaviour is a fact. It begins to look as if we'll have to admit that there's more than one kind of reality; that, in this particular case, there's something above and beyond the ordinary facts of men's behaviour, and yet quite definitely real—a real law, which none of us made, but which we find pressing on us.

IV

LET US sum up what we have reached so far. In the case of stones and trees and things of that sort, what we call the Laws of Nature may not be anything except a way of speaking. When you say that nature is governed by certain laws, this may only mean that nature does, in fact, behave in a certain way. The so-called laws may not be anything real— anything above and beyond the actual facts which we observe. But in the case of Man, we saw that this won't do. The law of Human Nature, or of Right and Wrong, must be something above and beyond the actual facts of human behaviour. In this case, besides the actual facts, you have something else—a real law which we didn't invent and which we know we ought to obey.

To-night I want to consider what this tells us about the universe we live in. Ever since men were able to think, they've been wondering what this universe really is and how it came to be there. And, very roughly, two views have been held. First, there is what is called the materialist view. People who take that view think that matter and space just happen to exist, and always have existed, nobody knows why; and that the matter, behaving in certain fixed ways, has just happened, by a sort of fluke, to produce creatures like ourselves who are able to think. By one chance in a thousand something hit our sun and made it produce the planets; and by another thousandth chance the chemicals necessary for life, and the right temperature, arose on one of these planets, and so some of the matter on this earth came alive; and then, by a very long series of chances, the living creatures developed into things like us. The other view is the religious view.[1] According to it, what is behind the universe is more like a mind than it's like anything else we know. That is to say, it's conscious, and has purposes, and prefers one thing to another. And on this view it made the universe, partly for purposes we don't know, but partly, at any rate, in order to produce creatures like itself—I mean, like itself to the extent of having minds. Please don't think that one of these views was held a long time ago and that the other has gradually taken its place. Wherever there have been thinking men both views turn up. And note this too. You can't find out which view is the right one by science in the ordinary sense. Science works by experiments. It watches how things behave. Every scientific statement in the long run, however complicated it looks, really means "I pointed the telescope to such and such a part of the sky at 2.20 A.M. on 15th January and saw so-and-so," or "I put some of this stuff in a pot and heated it to such-and-such a temperature and it did so-and-so." Don't think I'm saying anything against science: I'm only saying what its job is. And the more scientific a man is, the more (I believe) he'd agree with me that this is the job of science—and a very useful and necessary job it is too. But why anything comes to be there at all, and whether there's anything behind the things science observes—something of a different kind—this is not a scientific question. If there is "Something Behind," then either it will have to remain altogether unknown to men or else make itself known in some different way. The statement that there is any such thing, and the statement that there's

[1] See Note at the end of this Talk.

no such thing, are neither of them statements that science can make. And real scientists don't usually make them. It's usually the journalists and popular novelists who have picked up a few odds and ends of half-baked science from text-books who go in for them. After all, it's really a matter of common sense. Supposing science ever became complete so that it knew every single thing in the whole universe. Don't you see that the questions "Why is there a universe?" "Why does it go on as it does?" "Has it any meaning?" would remain just as they were?

Now the position would be quite hopeless but for this. There is one thing, and only one, in the whole universe which we know more about than we could learn from external observation. That one thing is Man. We don't merely ob-serve men, we *are* men. In this one case we have, so to speak, inside information; we're in the know. And because of that, we know that men find themselves under a moral law, which they didn't make, and can't quite forget even when they try, and which they know they ought to obey. Notice the follow-ing point. Anyone studying Man from the outside as we study electricity or cabbages, not knowing our language and consequently not able to get any inside knowledge from *us*, but merely observing what we did, would never get the slight-est evidence that we had this moral law. How could he? for his observations would only show what we did, and the moral law is about what we ought to do. In the same way, if there *is* anything above or behind the observed facts in the case of stones or the weather, we, by studying them from outside, could never hope .to discover it.

The position of the question, then, is like this. We want to know whether the universe simply happens to be what it is for no reason or whether there is a power behind it that makes it what it is. Since that power, if it exists, would be not one of the facts but a reality which makes the facts, no mere observation of the facts can find it. There's only one case in which we can know whether there's anything more, namely our own case. And in that one case we find there is. Or put it the other way round. If there was a controlling power outside the universe, it could not show itself to us as one of the facts inside the universe—no more than the architect of a house could actually be a wall or staircase or fireplace in that house. The only way in which we could expect it to show itself would be inside *us* as an influence or a command trying to get us to behave in a certain way. And that's just what we do find inside us. Doesn't it begin to look, if I may say so, very suspicious? In the only case where you can expect to get an answer, the answer turns out to be yes; and in the other cases, where you don't get an answer, you see *why* you don't. Suppose someone asked me, when I see a man in blue uniform going down the street leaving little paper packets at each house, why I suppose that they contain letters? I should reply, "Because whenever he leaves a similar little packet for me I find it does contain a letter." And if he then objected—"But you've never seen all these letters which you think the other people are getting," I should say, "Of course not, and I shouldn't expect to, because they're not addressed to me. I'm explaining the packets I'm not allowed to open by the ones I am allowed to open." It's the same about this question. The only packet I'm allowed to open is Man. When I do, especially when I open that particular man called Myself, I find that I don't exist on my own, that I'm under a law; that somebody or something wants me to behave in a certain way. I don't, of course, think that if I could get inside a stone or a tree I should find exactly the same thing, just as I don't think all the other people in the street get the *same* letters as I do. I should expect, for instance, to find that the stone *had* to obey the law of gravity—that whereas the sender of the letters merely tells me to do right, He *compels* the stone to obey the laws of its nature. But I should expect to find that there was, so to speak, a sender of letters in both cases, a Power behind the facts, a Director, a Guide.

Now don't think I'm going faster than I really am. I'm not yet within a hundred miles of the God of Christian theology. All I've got to is a Something which is directing the universe, and which appears in me as a law urging me to do right and making me feel responsible and uncomfortable when I do wrong. I think we have to assume it's more like a mind than it's like anything else we know—because after all the only other thing we know is matter and you can hardly imagine a bit of matter making a law. But, of course, it needn't be very like a mind, still less like a person. Next week we'll see if we can find out anything more about it. But one word of warning. There's been a great deal of soft soap talked about God for the last hundred years. That's not what I'm offering. You can cut all that out.

———

NOTE.—In order to keep this Talk short enough I mentioned only the Materialist view and the Religious view. But to be complete I ought to mention the In-between view called Life-Force philosophy, or Creative-Evolution, or Emergent Evolution. The wittiest expositions of it come in the works of Mr. G. B. Shaw, but the most profound ones in those of Bergson. People who hold this view say that the small variations by which life on this planet "evolved" from the lowest forms to Man were not due to chance but to the "striving" or "purposiveness" of a Life-Force. When people say this we must ask them whether by Life-Force they mean something with a mind or not. If they do, then "a mind bringing life into existence and leading it to perfection" is really a God, and their view is thus identical with the Religious. If they don't, then what is the sense in saying that something without a mind "strives" or has "purposes"? This seems to me fatal to their view. One reason why many people find Creative Evolution so attractive is that it gives one much of the emotional comfort of believing in God and none of the less pleasant consequences. When you are feeling fit and the sun is shining and you don't want to believe that the whole universe is a mere mechanical dance of atoms, it's nice to be able to think of this great mysterious Force rolling on through the centuries and carrying you on its crest. If, on the other hand, you want to do something rather shabby, the Life-Force being only a blind force, with no morals and no mind, will never interfere with you like that troublesome God we learned about when we were children. The Life-Force is a sort of *tame* God. *You* can switch *it* on when you want, but *it* won't bother *you*. All the thrills of religion and none of the cost. Is the Life-Force the greatest achievement of wishful thinking the world has yet seen?

V

I ENDED up last week with the idea that in the Moral Law somebody or something from beyond the material universe was actually getting at us. And I expect when I got that far some of you felt a certain annoyance. You may even have thought that I'd played a trick on you—that I'd been carefully wrapping up to look like philosophy what turns out to be one more "religious jaw." You may have felt you were ready to listen to me as long as you thought I'd anything new to say; but if it turns out to be only religion, well, the world's tried that and you can't put the clock back. If anyone is feeling that way I should like to say three things to him.

First, as to putting the clock back. Would you think I was joking if I said that you *can* put a clock back, and that if the clock is wrong it's often a very sensible thing to do? But I would rather get away from that whole idea of clocks. We all want progress. But progress means getting nearer to the place where you want to be. And if you've taken a wrong turning, then to go forward does *not* get you any nearer. If you're on the wrong road, progress means doing an about-turn and walking back to the right road; and in that case the man who turns back soonest is the most progressive man. We've all seen this at our jobs, haven't we? When I have started a bit of work the wrong way, the sooner I admit this and go back and start over again, the faster I shall get on. There's nothing progressive about being pig-headed and refusing to admit a mistake. And I think if you look at the present state of the world, it's pretty plain that humanity has been making some big mistake. We're on the wrong road. And if that is so, we must go back. Going *back* is the quickest way *on*.

Then secondly, this hasn't yet turned exactly into a religious talk. We haven't yet got as far as the God of any actual religion, still less the God of that particular religion called Christianity. We've only got as far as a Somebody or Something behind the Moral Law. We're not taking anything from the Bible or the Churches, we're trying to see what we can find out about this Somebody on our own steam. And I want to make it quite clear that what we find out on our own steam is something that gives us a shock. We have two bits of evidence about the Somebody. One is the universe He has made. If we used that as our only clue, then I think we should have to conclude that He was a great artist (for the universe is a very beautiful place), but also that He is quite merciless and no friend to man (for the universe is a very dangerous and terrifying place). The other bit of evidence is that Moral Law which He has put into our minds. And this is a better bit of evidence than the other, because it is inside information. You find out more about God from the Moral Law than from the universe in general just as you find out more about a man by listening to his conversation than by looking at a house he has built. Now, from this second bit of evidence we conclude that the Being behind the universe is intensely interested in right conduct—in fair play, unselfishness, and decency. In that sense we should agree with the account given by Christianity and some other religions, that God is "good." But do not let us go too fast here. The Moral Law doesn't give us any grounds for thinking that God is "good" in the sense of being indulgent, or soft, or sympathetic. There's nothing indulgent about the Moral Law. It's as hard as nails. It tells you to do the straight thing and it doesn't seem to care how painful, or dangerous, or difficult it is to do. If God is like the Moral Law then He is not soft. It's no use, at this stage, saying that what you mean by a "good" God is a God who can forgive. That's going too quickly. Only a Person can forgive. And we haven't yet got as far as a personal God—only as far as a power, behind the Moral Law, and more like a mind then it is like anything else. But it may still be very unlike a Person. If it is pure impersonal mind, there may be no sense in asking it to make allowances for you or let you off, just as there's no sense in asking the multiplication table to let you off when you do your sums wrong. You're *bound* to get the wrong answer. And it's no good either saying that if there is a God of that sort—an impersonal absolute goodness—then you don't like Him and aren't going to bother about Him. For the trouble is that part of you is on His side and really agrees with His disapproval of human greed and trickery and exploitation. You may want Him to make an exception in your own case, to let you off this one time; but you know at bottom that unless the power behind the world really and unalterably detests that sort of behaviour, then He can't be good. On the other hand, we know that if there does exist an absolute goodness it must hate most of what we do. That's the terrible fix we're in. If the universe is not governed by an absolute goodness, then all our efforts are in the long run hopeless. But if it is, then we are making ourselves enemies to that goodness every day, and aren't in the least likely to do any better to-morrow, and so our case is hopeless again. We can't do without it, and we can't do with it. God is the only comfort, He is also the supreme terror: the thing we most need and the thing we most want to keep out of the way of. He is our only possible ally, and we have made ourselves His enemies. Some people talk as if meeting the gaze of absolute goodness would be fun. They want to think again. They're still at the Munich stage of religion. Goodness is either the great safety or the great danger—according to the way you react to it. And we've reacted the wrong way.

Now my third point. When I chose to get to my real subject in this round-about way, I wasn't trying to play any
kind of trick on you. I had a different reason. My reason
was that Christianity simply doesn't make sense until you've
faced the sort of facts I've been describing. Christianity tells
people to repent and promises them forgiveness. It therefore has nothing (as far as I know) to say to people who
don't know they've done anything to repent of and who don't
feel that they need any forgiveness. It's after you've realised
that there is a real Moral Law, and a Power behind the law,
and that you have broken that law and put yourself wrong
with that Power—it's *after* all that that Christianity begins
to talk. When you know you're sick, you'll listen to the
doctor. When you have realised that our position is nearly
desperate you'll begin to understand what the Christians
are talking about. They offer an explanation of how we got
into our present state of both hating goodness and loving it.
They offer an explanation of how God can be this impersonal
mind at the back of the Moral Law and yet also a Person.
They tell you how the demands of this law, which you and
I can't meet, have been met on our behalf, how God Himself
becomes a man to save man from the disapproval of God. It's
an old story and if you want to go into it you will no doubt
consult people who have more authority to talk about it
than I have. All I'm doing is to get people to face the facts
—to understand the questions which Christianity claims to
answer. And they're very terrifying facts. I wish it were
possible, speaking in war-time, to say something more agree-
able. But I've got to say what I think true. Of course, I quite
agree that the Christian religion is, in the long run, a thing
of unspeakable comfort. But it doesn't begin in comfort; it
begins in the dismay I've been describing, and it's just no

good trying to go on to that comfort without first going through that dismay. In religion, as in the war and in everything else, comfort is the one thing you can't get by looking for it. If you're looking for truth, you may find comfort in the end: if you're looking for comfort you will not get *either* comfort *or* truth—only soft soap and wishful thinking to begin with and, in the end, despair. Most of us have got over the pre-war wishful thinking about international politics. It is time we did the same about religion.

Part II

WHAT CHRISTIANS BELIEVE

I

I HAVE been asked to tell you what Christians believe, and I am going to begin by telling you one thing that Christians don't need to believe. If you are a Christian you don't have to believe that all the other religions are simply wrong all through. If you are an atheist you do have to believe that the main point in all the religions of the whole world is simply one huge mistake. If you are a Christian, you are free to think that all these religions, even the queerest ones, contain at least some hint of the truth. When I was an atheist I had to try to persuade myself that the whole human race were pretty good fools until about one hundred years ago; when I became a Christian I was able to take a more liberal view. But, of course, being a Christian does mean thinking that where Christianity differs from other religions, Christianity is right and they are wrong. Like in arithmetic—there's only one right answer to a sum, and all other answers are wrong: but some of the wrong answers are much nearer being right than others.

The first big division of humanity is into the majority, who believe in some kind of God or gods, and the minority who don't. On this point, Christianity lines up with the majority—lines up with ancient Greeks and Romans, modern savages, Stoics, Platonists, Hindoos, Mohammedans, etc., against the modern Western European materialist. There are all sorts of different reasons for believing in God, and here I'll mention only one. It is this. Supposing there was no intelligence behind the universe, no creative mind. In that case nobody designed my brain for the purpose of thinking. It is merely that when the atoms inside my skull happen for physical or chemical reasons to arrange themselves in a certain way, this gives me, as a bye-product, the sensation I call thought. But if so, how can I trust my own thinking to be true? It's like upsetting a milk-jug and hoping that the way the splash arranges itself will give you a map of London. But if I can't trust my own thinking, of course I can't trust the arguments leading to atheism, and therefore have no reason to be an atheist, or anything else. Unless I believe in God, I can't believe in thought: so I can never use thought to disbelieve in God.

Now I go on to the next big division. People who all believe in God can be divided according to the sort of God they believe in. There are two very different ideas on this subject. One of them is the idea that He is beyond good and evil. *We* call one thing good and another thing bad. But according to some people that's merely our human point of view. These people would say that the wiser you become the less you'd want to call anything good or bad, and the more clearly you'd see that everything is good in one way and bad in another, and that nothing could have been different. Consequently, these people think that long before you got anywhere near the divine point of view the distinction would have disappeared altogether. We call a cancer bad, they'd say, because it kills a man; but you might just as well call a successful surgeon bad because he kills a cancer. It all depends on the point of view. The other and opposite idea

32

is that God is quite definitely "good" or "righteous," a God who takes sides, who loves love and hates hatred, who wants us to behave in one way and not in another. The first of these views—the one that thinks God beyond good and evil —is called Pantheism. It was held by the great Prussian philosopher Hegel and, as far as I can understand them, by the Hindoos. The other view is held by Jews, Mohammedans, and Christians.

And with this big difference between Pantheism and the Christian idea of God, there usually goes another. Pantheists usually believe that God, so to speak, animates the universe as you animate your body: that the universe almost *is* God, so that if it didn't exist He wouldn't exist either, and anything you find in the universe is a part of God. The Christian idea is quite different. They think God *made* the universe-- like a man making a picture or composing a tune. A painter isn't a picture, and he doesn't die if his picture is destroyed. You may say, "He's put a lot of himself into it," but that only means that all its beauty and interest has come out of his head. His skill isn't in the picture in the same way that it's in his head, or even in his hands. I expect you see how this difference between Pantheists and Christians hangs together with the other one. If you don't take the distinction between good and bad very seriously, then it's easy to say that anything you find in this world is a part of God. But, of course, if you think some things really bad, and God really good, then you can't talk like that. You must believe that God is separate from the world and that some of the things we see in it are contrary to His will. Confronted with a cancer or a slum the Pantheist can say, "If you could only see it from the divine point of view, you would realise that this also is God." The Christian replies, "Don't talk damned nonsense." [1] For Christianity is a fighting religion. It thinks God made the world—that space and time, heat and cold, and all the colours and tastes, and all the animals and vegetables, are things that God "made up out of His head" as a man makes up a story. But it also thinks that a great many things have gone wrong with the world that God made and that God insists, and insists very loudly, on our putting them right again.

And, of course, that raises a very big question. If a good God made the world why has it gone wrong? And for many years I simply wouldn't listen to the Christian answers to this question, because I kept on feeling "whatever you say, and however clever your arguments are, isn't it much simpler and easier to say that the world was *not* made by any intelligent power? Aren't all your arguments simply a complicated attempt to avoid the obvious?" But then that threw me back into those difficulties about atheism which I spoke of a moment ago. And soon I saw another difficulty.

My argument against God was that the universe seemed so cruel and unjust. But how had I got this idea of *just* and *unjust*? A man doesn't call a line crooked unless he has some idea of a straight line. What was I comparing this universe with when I called it unjust? If the whole show was bad and senseless from A to Z, so to speak, why did I, who was supposed to be part of the show, find myself in such violent reaction against it? A man feels wet when he falls into water, because man isn't a water animal: a fish wouldn't feel wet. Of course I could have given up my idea of justice by saying it was nothing but a private idea of my own. But if I did

[1] One listener complained of the word *damned* as frivolous swearing. But I mean exactly what I say—nonsense that is *damned* is under God's curse, and will (apart from God's grace) lead those who believe it to eternal death.

that then my argument against God collapsed too—for the argument depended on saying that the world was really un-just, not that it just didn't happen to please my private fancies. Thus in the very act of trying to prove that God didn't exist—in other words, that the whole of reality was senseless—I found I was forced to assume that one part of reality—namely my idea of justice—was full of sense. Consequently atheism turns out to be too simple. If the whole universe has no meaning, we should never have found out that it has no meaning: just as if there were no light in the universe and therefore no creatures with eyes we should never know it was dark. *Dark* would be a word without meaning.

II

VERY WELL then, atheism is too simple. And I'll tell you another view that is also too simple. It's the view I call Christianity-and-water, the view that just says there's a good God in Heaven and everything is all right—leaving out all the difficult and terrible doctrines about sin and hell and the devil, and the redemption. Both these are boys' philosophies.

It is no good asking for a simple religion. After all, real things *aren't* simple. They *look* simple, but they're not. The table I'm sitting at looks simple: but ask a scientist to tell you what it's really made of—all about the atoms and how the light waves rebound from them and hit my eye and what they do to the optic nerve and what it does to my brain—and, of course, you find that what we call "seeing a table"

35

lands you in mysteries and complications which you can hardly get to the end of. A child, saying a child's prayer, looks simple. And if you're content to stop there, well and good. But if you're not—and the modern world usually isn't —if you want to go on and ask what's really happening— then you must be prepared for something difficult. If we ask for something more than simplicity, it's silly then to complain that the something more isn't simple. Another thing I've noticed about reality is that, besides being difficult, it's odd: it isn't neat, it isn't what you expect. I mean, when you've grasped that the earth and the other planets all go round the sun, you'd naturally expect that all the planets were made to match—all at equal distances from each other, say, or distances that regularly increased, or all the same size, or else getting bigger or smaller as you go further from the sun. In fact, you find no rhyme or reason (that we can see) about either the sizes or the distances; and some of them have one moon, one has four, one has two, some have none, and one has a ring.

Reality, in fact, is always something you couldn't have guessed. That's *one* of the reasons I believe Christianity. It's a religion you couldn't have guessed. If it offered us just the kind of universe we'd always expected, I'd feel we were making it up. But, in fact, it's not the sort of thing anyone would have made up. It has just that queer twist about it that real things have. So let's leave behind all these boys' philosophies—these over-simple answers. The problem isn't simple and the answer isn't going to be simple either.

What is the problem? A universe that contains much that is obviously bad and apparently meaningless, but containing creatures like ourselves who know that it is bad and meaningless. There are only two views that face all the facts.

One is the Christian view that this is a good world that has gone wrong, but still retains the memory of what it ought to have been. The other is the view called Dualism. Dualism means the belief that there are two equal and independent powers at the back of everything, one of them good and the other bad, and that this universe is the battlefield in which they fight out an endless war. I personally think that next to Christianity Dualism is the manliest and most sensible creed on the market. But it has a catch in it.

The two powers, or spirits, or gods—the good one and the bad one—are supposed to be quite independent. They both existed from all eternity. Neither of them made the other, neither of them has any more right than the other to call itself God. Each presumably thinks it is good and thinks the other bad. One of them likes hatred and cruelty, the other likes love and mercy, and each backs its own view. Now what do we mean when we call one of them the Good Power and the other the Bad Power? Either we're merely saying that we happen to prefer the one to the other—like preferring beer to cider—or else we're saying that, whatever *they* say about it, and whichever *we* happen to like, one of them is actually wrong, actually mistaken, in regarding itself as good. Now if we mean merely that we happen to prefer the first, then we must give up talking about good and evil at all. For good means what you ought to prefer quite regardless of what you happen to like at any given moment. If "being good" meant simply joining the side you happened to fancy, for no real reason, then good wouldn't *be* good. So we must mean that one of the two powers is actually wrong and the other actually right.

But the moment you say that, you are putting into the universe a third thing in addition to the two Powers: some law or standard or rule of good which one of the powers conforms to and the other fails to conform to. But since the two powers are judged by this standard, then this standard, or the being who made this standard, is farther back and higher up than either of them, and He will be the real God. In fact, what we meant by calling them good and bad turns out to be that one of them is in a right relation to the real ultimate God and the other in a wrong relation to Him.

The same point can be made in a different way. If Dualism is true, then the Bad Power must be a being who likes badness for its own sake. But in reality we have no experience of anyone liking badness just because it is bad. The nearest we can get to it is in cruelty. But in real life people are cruel for one of two reasons—either because they are sadists, that is, because they have a sexual perversion which makes cruelty a cause of sensual pleasure to them, or else for the sake of something they are going to get out of it—money, or power, or safety. But pleasure, money, power, and safety are all, as far as they go, good things. The badness consists in pursuing them by the wrong method, or in the wrong way, or too much. I don't mean, of course, that the people who do this aren't desperately wicked. I do mean that wickedness, when you examine it, turns out to be the pursuit of some good in the wrong way. You can be good for the mere sake of goodness: you can't be bad for the mere sake of badness. You can do a kind action when you're not feeling kind and when it gives you no pleasure, simply because kindness is right; but no one ever did a cruel action simply because cruelty is wrong—only because cruelty was pleasant or useful to him. In other words badness can't succeed even in being bad *in the same way* in which goodness is good. Goodness is, so to speak, itself: badness is only spoiled goodness. And there must be something good first before it can be spoiled. We called Sadism a sexual perversion; but you must first have the idea of a normal sexuality before you can talk of it being perverted; and you can see which is the perversion, because you can explain the perverted from the normal, and can't explain the normal from the perverted. It follows that the Bad Power, who is supposed to be on an equal footing with the Good Power, and to love badness in the same way as the good one loves goodness, is a mere bogey. In order to be bad he must have good things to want and then to pursue in the wrong way: he must have impulses which were originally good in order to be able to pervert them. But if he is bad he can't supply himself either with good things to desire or with good impulses to pervert. He must be getting both from the Good Power. And if so, then he is not independent. He is part of the Good Power's world: he was made either by the Good Power or by some power above them both.

Put it more simply still. To be bad, he must exist and have intelligence and will. But existence, intelligence, and will are in themselves good. Therefore he must be getting them from the Good Power: even to be bad he must borrow or steal from his opponent. And do you now begin to see why Christianity has always said that the devil is a fallen angel? That isn't a mere story for the children. It's a real recognition of the fact that evil is a parasite, not an original thing. The powers which enable evil to carry on are powers given it by goodness. All the things which enable a bad man to be effectively bad are in themselves good things—resolution, cleverness, good looks, existence itself. That's why Dualism, in a strict sense, won't work.

But I want to say that real Christianity (as distinct from

Christianity-and-water) goes much nearer to Dualism than people think. One of the things that surprised me when I first read the New Testament seriously was that it was always talking about a Dark Power in the universe—a mighty evil spirit who was held to be the Power behind death and disease, and sin. The difference is that Christianity thinks this Dark Power was created by God, and was good when he was created, and went wrong. Christianity agrees with Dualism that this universe is at war. But it doesn't think this is a war between independent powers. It thinks it's a civil war, a rebellion, and that we are living in a part of the universe occupied by the rebel.

Enemy-occupied territory—that's what this world is. Christianity is the story of how the rightful king has landed, you might say landed in disguise, and is calling us all to take part in a great campaign of sabotage. When you go to church you're really listening in to the secret wireless from our friends: that's why the enemy is so anxious to prevent us going. He does it by playing on our conceit and laziness and intellectual snobbery. I know someone will ask me, "Do you really mean, at this time of day, to re-introduce our old friend the devil—hoofs and horns and all?" Well, what the time of day has to do with it I don't know. And I'm not particular about the hoofs and horns. But in other respects my answer is, "Yes, I do." I don't claim to know anything about his personal appearance. If anybody really wants to know him better I'd say to that person, "Don't worry. If you really want to, you will. Whether you'll like it when you do is another question."

III

CHRISTIANS, then, believe that an evil power has made himself for the present the Prince of this World. And, of course, that raises problems. Is this state of affairs in accordance with God's will or not? If it is, He's a strange God, you'll say: and if it isn't, how *can* anything happen contrary to the will of a being with absolute power?

But anyone who has been in authority knows how a thing can be in accordance with your will in one way and not in another. It may be quite sensible for a mother to say to the children, "I'm not going to go and make you tidy the schoolroom every night. You've got to learn to keep it tidy on your own." Then she goes up one night and finds the Teddy bear and the ink and the French Grammar all lying in the grate. That's against her will. She would prefer the children to be tidy. But on the other hand, it is her will which has left the children free to be untidy. The same thing arises in any regiment, or trades union, or school. You make a thing voluntary and then half the people don't do it. That isn't what you willed, but your will has made it possible.

It's probably the same in the universe. God created things which had free will. That means creatures which can go wrong *or* right. Some people think they can imagine a creature which was free but had no possibility of going wrong, but I can't. If a thing is free to be good it's also free to be bad. And free will is what has made evil possible. Why, then, did God give them free will? Because free will, though it makes evil possible, is also the only thing that makes possible any love or goodness or joy worth having. A world of automata—of creatures that worked like machines—would hardly be worth creating. The happiness which God designs for His higher creatures is the happiness of being freely, voluntarily united to Him and to each other in an ecstasy of love and delight compared with which the most rapturous love between a man and a woman on this earth is *mere milk and water*. And for that they've got to be free.

Of course God knew that would happen if they used their freedom the wrong way: apparently He thought it worth the risk. Perhaps we feel inclined to disagree with Him. But there's a difficulty about disagreeing with God. He is the source from which all your reasoning power comes: you couldn't be right and He wrong any more than a stream can rise higher than its own source. When you are arguing against Him you're arguing against the very power that makes you able to argue at all: it's like cutting off the branch you're sitting on. If God thinks this state of war in the universe a price worth paying for free will—that is, for making a *real* world in which creatures can do real good or harm and something of real importance can happen, instead of a toy world which only moves when He pulls the strings—then we may take it it *is* worth paying.

When we've understood about free will, we shall see how silly it is to ask, as somebody once asked me: "Why did God make a creature of such rotten stuff that it went wrong?" The better stuff a creature is made of—the cleverer and stronger and freer it is—then the better it will be if it goes right, but also the worse it will be if it goes wrong. A cow can't be very good or very bad; a dog can be both better and worse; a child better and worse still; an ordinary man, still more so; a man of genius, still more so; a super-human spirit best—or worst—of all.

How did the Dark Power go wrong? Well, the moment you have a self at all, there is a possibility of putting yourself first—wanting to be the centre—wanting to *be* God, in fact. That was the sin of Satan: and that was the sin he taught the human race. Some people think the fall of man had something to do with sex, but that's a mistake. What Satan put into the heads of our remote ancestors was the idea that they could "be like gods"—could set up on their own as if they had created themselves—be their own masters —invent some sort of happiness for themselves outside God, apart from God. And out of that hopeless attempt has come nearly all that we call human history—money, poverty, am-bition, war, prostitution, classes, empires, slavery—the long terrible story of man trying to find something other than God which will make him happy.

The reason why it can never succeed is this. God made us: invented us as a man invents an engine. A car is made to run on petrol, and it won't run properly on anything else. Now God designed the human machine to run on Himself. He Himself is the fuel our spirits were designed to burn, or the food our spirits were designed to feed on. There isn't any other. That's why it's just no good asking God to make us happy in our own way without bothering about religion. God can't give us a happiness and peace apart from Him-self, because it isn't there. There's no such thing.

That is the key to history. Terrific energy is expended— civilisations are built up—excellent institutions devised; but each time something goes wrong. Some fatal flaw always brings the selfish and cruel people to the top and it all slides back into misery and ruin. In fact, the machine konks. It seems to start up all right and runs a few yards, and then it breaks down. They're trying to run it on the wrong juice. That's what Satan has done to us humans.

And what did God do? First of all He left us conscience, the sense of right and wrong: and all through history there have been people trying (some of them very hard) to obey it. None of them ever quite succeeded. Secondly, He sent the human race what I call good dreams: I mean those queer stories scattered all through the heathen religions about a god who dies and comes to life again and, by his death, has somehow given new life to men. Thirdly, He selected one particular people and spent several centuries hammering into their heads the sort of God He was—that there was only one of Him and that He cared about right conduct. Those people were the Jews, and the Old Testament gives an account of the hammering process.

Then comes the real shock. Among these Jews there suddenly turns up a man who goes about talking as if He was God. He claims to forgive sins. He says He has always existed. He says He is coming to judge the world at the end of time. Now let us get this clear. Among Pantheists, like the Indians, anyone might say that he was a part of God, or one with God: there'd be nothing very odd about it. But this man, since He was a Jew, couldn't mean that kind of God. God, in their language, meant the Being outside the world Who had made it and was infinitely different from anything else. And when you've grasped that, you will see that what this man said was, quite simply, the most shocking thing that has ever been uttered by human lips.

I'm trying here to prevent anyone from saying the really silly thing that people often say about Him: "I'm ready to accept Jesus as a great moral teacher, but I don't accept His claim to be God." That's the one thing we mustn't say. A man who was merely a man and said the sort of things Jesus said wouldn't be a great moral teacher. He'd either be a lunatic—on a level with the man who says he's a poached egg—or else he'd be the Devil of Hell. You must make your choice. Either this man was, and is, the Son of God: or else a madman or something worse. You can shut Him up for a fool, you can spit at Him and kill Him as a demon; or you can fall at His feet and call Him Lord and God. But don't let us come with any patronising nonsense about His being a great human teacher. He hasn't left that open to us. He didn't intend to.

IV

WE ARE faced, then, with a frightening alternative. This man we're talking about either was (and is) just what He said or else a lunatic, or something worse. Now it seems to me obvious that He wasn't either a lunatic or a fiend: and consequently, however strange or terrifying or unlikely it may seem, I have to accept the view that He was and is God. God has landed on this enemy-occupied world in human form.

And now, what was the purpose of it all? What did He come to do? Well, to teach, of course; but as soon as you look into the New Testament or any other Christian writing you'll find they're constantly talking about something different—about His death and His coming to life again. It's obvious that Christians think the whole point of the story lies there. They think the main thing He came to earth to do was to suffer and be killed.

Now before I became a Christian I was under the impression that the main thing Christians had to believe was one particular theory as to what the point of this dying was. According to that theory God wanted to punish men for having deserted and joined the Great Rebel, but Christ volunteered to be punished instead, and so God let us off. Now I admit that even this theory doesn't seem to me quite so immoral and so silly as it used to; but that isn't the point I want to make. What I came to see later on was that neither this theory nor any other *is* Christianity. The central Christian belief is that Christ's death has somehow put us right with God and given us a fresh start. Theories as to *how* it did this are another matter. A good many different theories have been held as to how it works; what all Christians are agreed on is that it does work. I'll tell you what I think it's like. All sensible people know that if you're tired and hungry a meal will do you good. But the modern theory of nourishment—all about the vitamins and proteins—is a different thing. People ate their dinners and felt better long before the theory of vitamins was ever heard of: and if the theory of vitamins is some day abandoned they'll go on eating their dinners just the same. Theories about Christ's death aren't Christianity: they're explanations about how it works. Christians wouldn't all agree as to how important these theories are. My own church—the Church of England—doesn't lay down any one of them as the right one. The Church of Rome goes a bit further. But I think they'll all agree that the

46

thing itself is infinitely more important than any explanations that theologians have produced. I think they'd probably admit that no explanation will ever be quite adequate
to the reality. But as I said in the preface to this book, I'm
only a layman, and at this point we're getting into deep
water. So I'll just tell you, for what it's worth, how I personally look at the matter.

On my view the theories are not themselves the thing
you're asked to accept. I wonder have many of you read
Jeans or Eddington? What they do when they want to explain the atom, or something of that sort, is to give you a
description out of which you can make a mental picture.
But then they warn you that this picture is not what the scientists actually believe. What the scientists believe is a math-
ematical formula. The pictures are there only to help you
to understand the formula. They are not really true in the
way the formula is; they don't give you the real thing but
only something more or less like it. They're only meant to
help, and if they don't help you can drop them. The thing
itself *can't* be pictured, it can only be expressed mathemati-
cally. Now we're in the same boat here. We believe that the
death of Christ is just that point in history at which something absolutely unimaginable from outside shows through
into our own world. And if we can't picture even the atoms
of which our own world is built, of course we're not going
to be able to picture this. Indeed, if we found that we could
fully understand it, that very fact would show it wasn't what
it professes to be—the inconceivable, the uncreated, the
thing from beyond nature, striking down into nature like
lightning. You may ask what good will it be to us if we
don't understand it. But that's an easy one. A man can eat
his dinner without understanding exactly how food nour-

ishes him. A man can accept what Christ has done without knowing how it works: indeed, he certainly won't know how it works *until* he's accepted it.

We are told that Christ was killed for us, that His death has washed out our sins, and that by dying He disabled death itself. That's the formula. That's Christianity. That's what has to be believed. Any theories we build up as to how Christ's death did all this are, in my view, quite secondary: mere plans or diagrams to be left alone if they don't help us, and, even if they do help us, not to be confused with the thing itself. All the same, some of these theories are worth looking at.

The one most people have heard is the one I mentioned before—the one about our being let off because Christ had volunteered to bear a punishment instead of us. Now on the face of it that's a very silly theory. If God was prepared to let us off, why on earth didn't He do so? And what possible point could there be in punishing an innocent person instead? None at all that I can see if you're thinking of punishment in the police-court sense. On the other hand, if you think of a debt, there's plenty of point in a person who has some assets paying it on behalf of someone who hasn't. Or if you take "paying the penalty," not in the sense of being punished, but in the more general sense of standing the racket or footing the bill, then, of course, it's a matter of common experience that, when one person has got himself into a hole, the trouble of getting him out usually falls on a kind friend.

Now what was the sort of "hole" man had got himself into? He had tried to set up on his own, to behave as if he belonged to himself. In other words, fallen man isn't simply

48

an imperfect creature who needs improvement: he's a rebel who must lay down his arms. Laying down your arms, surrendering, saying you're sorry, realising that you've been on the wrong track and getting ready to start life over again from the ground floor—that's the only way out of our "hole." This process of surrender—this movement full speed astern—is what Christians call repentance. Now repentance isn't any fun at all. It's something much harder than just eating humble pie. It means unlearning all the self-conceit and self-will that we've been training ourselves into for thousands of years. It means *killing* part of yourself, undergoing a kind of death. In fact it needs a good man to repent. And here comes the catch. Only a bad person *needs* to repent: only a good person *can* repent. The worse you are the more you need it and the less you can do it. The only person who could do it perfectly would be a perfect person—and he wouldn't need it.

Remember, this repentance, this willing submission to humiliation and a kind of death, isn't something God demands of you before He'll take you back and which He could let you off if He chose: it's simply a description of what going back to Him is like. If you ask God to take you back without it, you're really asking Him to let you go back without going back. It can't happen. Very well, then, we've got to go through with it. But the same badness which makes us need it, makes us unable to do it. Can we do it if God helps us? Yes, but what do we mean when we talk of God helping us? We mean God putting into us a bit of Himself, so to speak. He lends us a little of His reasoning powers and that's how we think: He puts a little of His love into us and that's how we love one another. When you teach a child writing, you hold its hand while it forms the letters: that is, it

49

forms the letters because you are forming them. We love and reason because God loves and reasons and holds our hand while we do it. Now if we hadn't fallen, that would be all plain sailing. But unfortunately we now need God's help in order to do something which God, in His own nature, never does at all—to surrender, to suffer, to submit, to die. Nothing in God's nature corresponds to this process at all. So that the one road for which we now need God's leadership most of all is a road God, in His own nature, has never walked. God can share only what He has: this thing, in His own nature, He has not.

But supposing God became a man—suppose our human nature which can suffer and die was amalgamated with God's nature in one person—then that person could help us. He could surrender His will, and suffer and die, because He was man; and He could do it perfectly because He was God. You and I can go through this process only if God does it in us; but God can do it only if He becomes man. Our attempts at this dying will succeed only if we men share in God's dying, just as our thinking can succeed only because it is a drop out of the ocean of His intelligence: but we can't share God's dying unless God dies; and He can't die except by being a man. That is the sense in which He pays our debt, and suffers for us what He Himself needn't suffer at all.

At least that's how I see it. But remember this is only one more picture. Don't mistake it for the thing itself: and if it doesn't help you, drop it.

V

THE PERFECT surrender and humiliation was undergone by Christ: perfect because He was God, surrender and humiliation because He was man. Now the Christian belief is that if we somehow share the humility and suffering of Christ we shall also share in His conquest of death and find a new life after we have died and in it become perfect, and perfectly happy, creatures. This means something much more than our trying to follow His teaching. People often ask when the next step in evolution—the step to something beyond man—will happen. Well, on the Christian view, it has happened already. In Christ, a new kind of man appeared: and the new kind of life which began in Him is to be put into us.

How is this to be done? Now, please remember how we acquired the old, ordinary kind of life. We derived it from others, from our father and mother and all our ancestors, without our consent—and by a very curious process, involving pleasure, pain, and danger. A process you'd never have guessed. Most of us spend a good many years in childhood trying to guess it: and some children, when they're first told, don't believe it—and I'm not sure that I blame them, for it *is* very odd. Now the God who arranged that process is the same God who arranges how the new kind of life—the Christ life—is to be spread. So you must be prepared for it being odd too. He didn't consult us when He invented sex: He hasn't consulted us either when He invented this.

There are three things that spread the Christ life to us: baptism, belief, and that mysterious action which different Christians call by different names—Holy Communion, the Mass, the Lord's Supper. At least, those are the three ordinary methods. I'm not saying there may not be special cases where it is spread without one or more of these. I haven't time to go into special cases, and I don't know enough. If you're trying in a few minutes to tell a man how to get to Edinburgh you'll tell him the trains: he *can* get there by boat or by a plane, but you'd hardly bring that in. And I'm not saying anything about which of these three things is the most essential. My Methodist friend would like me to say a lot more about belief and a lot less (in proportion) about the other two. But I'm not going into that. Anyone who professes to teach you Christian doctrine will, in fact, tell you to use all three, and that's good enough for our present purpose.

I can't myself see why these things should be the conductors of the new kind of life. But then, if one didn't happen to know, I should never have seen any connection between a particular physical pleasure and the appearance of a new human being in the world. We've got to take reality as it comes to us: there's no good jabbering about what it ought to be like or what we'd have expected it to be like. But though I can't see why it *should* be so, I can tell you why I believe it *is* so. I've explained why I have to believe that Jesus was (and is) God. And it seems plain as a matter of history that He taught His followers that the new life was communicated in this way. In other words, I believe it on His authority. Don't be scared by the word authority.

Believing things on authority only means believing them because you've been told them by someone you think trustworthy. Ninety-nine per cent. of the things you believe are believed on authority. I believe there is such a place as New York. I haven't seen it myself. I couldn't prove by abstract reasoning that there must be such a place. I believe it because reliable people have told me so. The ordinary man believes in the Solar System, atoms, evolution, and the circulation of the blood on authority—because the scientists say so. Every historical statement in the world is believed on authority. None of us has seen the Norman Conquest or the defeat of the Armada. None of us could prove them by pure logic as you prove a thing in mathematics. We believe them simply because people who did see them have left writings that tell us about them: in fact, on authority. A man who jibbed at authority in other things as some people do in religion would have to be content to know nothing all his life.

Don't think I'm setting up baptism and belief and the Holy Communion as things that will do instead of your own attempts to copy Christ. Your natural life is derived from your parents; that doesn't mean it will stay there if you do nothing about it. You can lose it by neglect, or you can drive it away by committing suicide. You've got to feed it and look after it: but remember, all the time you're not making it you're only keeping up a life you got from someone else. In the same way a Christian can lose the Christ-life which has been put into him, and he has to make efforts to keep it. But even the best Christian that ever lived is not acting on his own steam—he is only nourishing or protecting a life he could never have acquired by his own efforts. And that has practical consequences. As long as the natural life is in your body, it will do a lot towards repairing that body. Cut it, and up to a point it will heal, as a dead body wouldn't. A live body isn't one that never gets hurt, but one that can to some extent repair itself. In the same way a Christian isn't a man who never goes wrong, but a man who is enabled to repent and pick himself up and begin over again after each stumble—because the Christ-life is inside him, repairing him all the time, enabling him to repeat (in some degree) the kind of voluntary death which Christ Himself carried out.

That is why the Christian is in a different position from other people who are trying to be good. They hope, by being good, to please God if there is one; or—if they think there isn't—at least they hope to deserve approval from good men. But the Christian thinks any good he does comes from the Christ-life inside him. He doesn't think God will love us because we're good, but that God will make us good because He loves us; just as the roof of a greenhouse doesn't attract the sun because it's bright, but becomes bright because the sun shines on it.

And let me make it quite clear that when Christians say the Christ-life is in them, they don't mean simply something mental or moral. This isn't simply a way of saying that we are thinking about Christ or copying Him. They mean that Christ is actually operating through them; that the whole mass of Christians are literally the physical organism through which Christ acts—that we are His fingers and muscles, the cells of His body. And perhaps that explains one or two things. It explains why this new life is spread not only by purely mental acts like belief, but by bodily acts like baptism and Holy Communion. It's not merely the spreading of an idea; it's more like evolution—a biological or super-biological fact. There's no good trying to be more spiritual than God. God never meant man to be a purely spiritual creature. That's why He uses material things like bread and wine to put the new life into us. We may think this rather crude and unspiritual. God doesn't: He *invented* eating. He likes matter. He invented it.

Then there's another thing that used to puzzle me. Isn't it frightfully unfair that this new life should be confined to people who have heard of Christ and been able to believe in Him? Well, the truth is God hasn't told us what His arrangements about the other people are. We do know that no man can be saved except through Christ; we don't know that only those who know Him can be saved through Him. But in the meantime, if you're worried about the people outside, the most unreasonable thing you can do is to remain outside yourself. Christians are Christ's body, the organism through which He works. Every addition to that body enables Him to do more. If you want to help those outside you must add your own little cell to the body of Christ who *can* help them. Cutting off a man's fingers would be an odd way of getting him to do more work.

Another possible objection is this: Why is God landing in this enemy-occupied world in disguise and starting a sort of secret society to undermine the devil? Why isn't he landing in force, invading it? Is it that He isn't strong enough? Well, Christians think He's going to land in force; we don't know when. But we can guess why He's delaying. He wants to give us the chance of joining His side freely. I don't suppose you and I would think much of a Frenchman who waited till the Allies were marching into Berlin and then announced he was on our side. God will invade. But I wonder whether people who ask God to interfere openly and directly in our world quite realise what it will be like when

He does. When that happens, it's the end of the world. When the author walks on to the stage the play's over. God's going to invade, all right: but what's the good of saying you're on His side *then*, when you see the whole natural universe melting away like a dream and something else—something it never entered your head to conceive—comes crashing in; something so beautiful to some of us and so terrible to others that none of us will have any choice left? For this time it will be God *without* disguise; something so overwhelming that it will strike either irresistible love or irresistible horror into every creature. It will be too late then to *choose* your side. There's no good saying you choose to lie down when it has become impossible to stand up. That won't be the time for choosing: it will be the time when we discover which side we really have chosen, whether we realised it before or not. *Now* is our chance to choose the right side. God is holding back to give us that chance. It won't last for ever. We must take it or leave it.